Secrets of the Show Cars

Published by
Michael Bruce Associates, Inc.
Post Office Box 396
Powell, Ohio 43065

CONTENTS

Credits: Cover Photography by Mike Antonick. Cover design by Dick Yoakam and Mike Antonick. Cover car owned by Paul Kitchen. Text by Mike Antonick with Dave Burroughs. Technical consultation by Milt Antonick, John Amgwert, Dave Burroughs, Bill Munzer and Don Williams. Graphics by Mike Antonick.

FIRST PRINTING

Chapter One

First Things First

The care and affection lavished upon automobiles is nothing less than astonishing, especially to those people at the opposite end of the spectrum who view a car as nothing more than a means of getting between two points, and a not altogether enjoyable means at that.

There is no point in attempting to explain this "love of cars" phenomenon. If you are reading this text, you have some understanding of it. And if you're like most enthusiasts, more know-how is what you're really seeking. You may want to maintain your new or near-new car in its present condition. Or you may want to refurbish your car and then keep it pristine. The point is that you know where you want to be, but you may not know all the steps involved in getting there.

Despite the title of this book, its sole purpose is not to provide a road map for success on the show car circuit. It can certainly be helpful in that regard, but its real intent is to tap the vast knowledge of those who do show autos, because the "secrets" these people possess can be used to reach any number of different goals. At one extreme is the person who wants nothing more than to spend a weekend making his everyday "driver" look as good as it possibly can. At the other end is the owner who is intent on creating a museum piece, a car that is literally too good to drive.

No one who has attended a showing of beautifully prepared automobiles can come away without wondering at least a few times how certain effects or tasks were accomplished. Some come away thinking that all that's involved is a lot of sweat and patience, but no great amount of skill or knowhow.

Well, it is true that many show car tricks are self-taught with experience, but skill and a knowledge of the techniques are very important aspects of a successful car preparation. The importance of knowing what to do and how to do it cannot be overstated. When you get right down to it, most people don't even know how to properly wash a car, let alone how to refurbish, maintain, and preserve it.

Saying that most people don't know how to wash a car can be dangerously misinterpreted. The statement is true, but saying it sounds pompous. After all, no one knows it all. The people who provided the consultation for *Secrets of the Show Cars* are among the best. The techniques and the products they use work and work well. But this shouldn't be taken as gospel written in stone. Others use different techniques and products to achieve equal, maybe even better results. Like all sciences, the science of car care is constantly improving with the discovery of new techniques and the introduction of new products. For instance, it wasn't very long ago that silicone brake fluid didn't exist. Its proper use now can virtually eliminate the brake problems that drove car enthusiasts nuts just a few years ago.

Also changing is the intent of auto restoration and preservation. At one time the goal was pure perfection. Perfection

In many circles, perfection is now beginning to mean preservation of a car as it was originally built.

is still the goal, but the definition of perfection is changing. Perfection used to mean just what the word implies . . . flawless, gleaming parts with not a ragged edge or scratch to be found. But in many circles, perfection is now beginning to mean the preservation or restoration of a car as it was originally built. The "perfect" car would then be one that was a duplicate of the same car rolling off the original assembly line, flaws and all. The whole idea is the preservation of a car's identity and its character.

Many novices make the mistake of thinking that they will enhance the value of their car by "stripping" it and starting over. Using the engine compartment as an example, they would take everything down to bare metal, repainting, polishing, or replating everything. Looks pretty, but in the eyes of the collector, the car's value might go down, not up. Because in the process of "cleaning" the car up, much of the car's history, identity, and authenticity has been erased forever.

This is a very important concept to understand. A few years ago, a book like *Secrets of the Show Cars* would have stated flatly that the first thing to do in an engine compartment was to steam clean it. Something like lacquer thinner would have been recommended to clean up anything the steaming missed.

Steam cleaning can certainly be helpful and lacquer thinner is indispensable for a number of tasks. But state-of-the-art in car care demands that you put them on the back shelf unless absolutely necessary. That greasy engine you're tempted to turn the steam wand on may have scores of decals, labels and code markings intact under the crud that will be lifted off and they'll roll right down the floor vent with the dirt. Any used car lot can steam an engine and make it look cosmetically nice with a couple of spray bombs. How much more impressive to find a relic that is intact with original factory applied details. Any investment-minded enthusiast would prefer the original car with a few chips, than the reworked one with everything glossed over. The message here is caution and consideration for what you want to achieve.

Most of the tips appearing in this book can be applied to any type of car. The photos were staged using a nice mid-sixties Oldsmobile, a nearly new Cadillac, and several Corvettes. The people who provided the expertise tended to be Corvette-oriented, but again, the information is largely transferable.

All the photos appearing in this book were taken by Mike Antonick who also wrote the text. The staging for the photos was done by Dave Burroughs and Mike Antonick. Dave Burroughs provided much of the technical expertise. Additional technical input was provided by John Amgwert, Milt Antonick, Bill Munzer, and Don Williams.

The credentials of these men are impressive. Dave Burroughs is an aviation enthusiast who also happens to have a passion for "mid-year" Corvettes, those built between 1963 and 1967. Dave began his teen summers working at a small local airport, mowing grass and generally poking around the aircraft for $50 and an hour's free flying time a week, and after formal maintenance and flying training spent five years as a professional pilot.

Airplane people tend to be fussy. They had better be, because with airplanes there isn't much room for error. Dave carried these traits along when he entered the show car circuit. In 1976, his silver 1967 Corvette became the first Corvette to win the "triple crown" with class wins at what were then the big three Corvette national shows. They were *Bloomington* in Illinois, *McDorman's* in Ohio, and the *National Council of Corvette Clubs* national meet held that year in Orlando, Florida.

In 1978, Dave Burroughs conceived and organized the National Corvette Certification Board for judging Corvettes which is now used at the Bloomington show. He has also

---

A restoration now considered to be at the pinnacle of state-of-the-art in restoration correctness.

---

recently completed a 4000 hour, three-year restoration of a 1965 Corvette that is considered by those in the know to be at the pinnacle of state-of-the-art in restoration correctness.

Bill Munzer and Don Williams also have Corvette concours experience. Bill tends to concentrate on chassis/engine and interior work, while Don is an artist with exterior body repair and refinishing. The two men have pooled their talents in the past to create breathtaking and successful show cars that have won more awards than they can keep track of, and thousands of dollars in prize money. One of their joint show projects, a 1963 fuel-injected Corvette, won them a brand new Corvette at the McDorman show in central Ohio. Not bad.

John Amgwert was one of the seven original founders of the *National Corvette Restorers Society* in 1974. Since then, he's been the editor and publisher of *The Corvette Restorer,* the NCRS's quarterly magazine. He's also written restoration articles for such publications as *Hot Rod* and *Corvette News,* and has participated in countless concours events as judge, entrant, and organizer.

Milt Antonick is an industrial designer with heavy auto experience. He was with Studebaker when the Avanti was done, and he did much of the Avanti's interior renderings. While at Chrysler, Antonick headed the design groups responsible for such marketing successes as the Duster and Barracuda. He financed his education by winning the top national award in GM's Fisher Body Craftsmans Guild contest for auto design and building. Antonick loves all sorts of cars and offers not only his personal expertise, but also that gleaned from the internal modeling shops of the major automakers.

There are many other people from whom these men have learned. Enthusiasts like Don Ellefsen, Sam Folz, Cliff Gottlob, Mike Hansen, Mike Ilyin, Paul Kitchen, Jim Krughoff, Bill Locke, Dr. Bill Miller, Chip Miller, Bill Mock, Errol McKoy, Jim Otto, Jim Prather, Chuck Rossmann, and Dale Smith. To the many not mentioned, our apologies.

Most concours experts are reluctant to reveal their secrets. It's not because they don't want others to know how they do what they do; just the opposite is generally true. The

---

They're always on the prowl for some little bit of expertise they can add to their repertoire.

---

basis for the reluctance is that these people don't enjoy being preachy. They'll never say something has to be done a certain way, though there are some definite taboos. Most often, these people spend their time listening, not lecturing. They're always on the prowl for some little bit of expertise they can add to their repertoire.

Excluding a few who make their living detailing cars, those knowledgeable in show car preparation do what they do because they enjoy it. They don't care whether you care or not. They're almost always low-key types who enjoy talking about their craft only to people who genuinely enjoy hearing what they have to say.

When the information does start to flow from these people, it comes in gushes. They've forgotten more than most of us ever knew about detailing a car. They have tricks and techniques developed or picked up over the years that they just do instinctively. But as they unload their warehouse of data, a familiar disclaimer keeps being inserted. It goes something like this: "Now, this is the way I do it, but that doesn't mean there aren't faster or better ways. I just like this way because . . . "

The same sort of disclaimer applies to the products pictured and mentioned throughout *Secrets of the Show Cars*. The consulting pros use and like the products shown and they definitely work for the effects they're trying to achieve. But that's as far as our endorsement goes. There are certainly other products that are as good, maybe better. The manufacturers are all receiving free plugs. None of them knew in advance that their wares would be mentioned in this text, and some would probably object to some of the unorthodox product uses the pros dream up anyway.

Getting Started

No matter how much or little you intend to do to your car, a good first step is to photograph what you're starting with before you do anything else. This is helpful for two reasons: First, there will be some disassembly involved somewhere along the way and having "before" photos can prove invaluable for later reference. A lot can be taken for granted during disassembly. Things that come apart easily and logically sometimes don't go back together with the same ease and logic. Carburetor hookup and linkage on newer cars is a good example of something that comes apart easier than it goes back together. There are lots of other things far less obvious. Was this little widgit held on with a phillips head or slotted

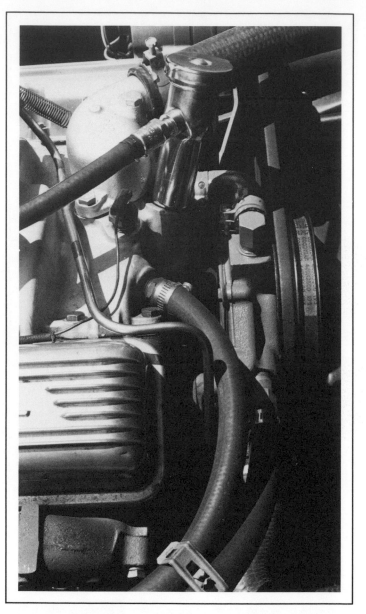

Documentation photos serve two purposes. First, a history of the car before and during refurbishing is established. Second, photos can assist greatly during reassembly. Note at left the details of the forward engine area. Carburetor and linkage are shown above.

screw? Was this clamp on the upper or lower end of the hose? This bracket fits back on a couple of different ways, so which way is right? Was this clip painted or raw?

A second reason for the photos is simply to permanently record what you started with. Maybe the car is not being detailed for resale, but it doesn't hurt to pretend it is anyway. Put yourself in the shoes of a prospective buyer looking at an immaculately detailed automobile.

Anyone looking at cosmetic perfection instinctively asks himself, "What was it before? Was it a wreck skillfully pieced together?" There may not be anything wrong with that, but if you started with a nice straight car and just made it better, doesn't it make sense to have that adequately documented?

Articles on classic car care and restoration often recommend buying one of the inexpensive instant cameras to do your photo documentation. We can only conclude that these folks haven't tried what they're recommending because the cheap instants do a lousy job. These cameras are equipped with lenses designed for what most people buying this type of camera will use it for. That means a fairly wide angle shot of the family gathered around the Christmas tree, not engine detail shots. In order to get in close on something like carburetor linkage, you'll need to upgrade to a much better

> *This type of camera is good for a shot of the family gathered around the Christmas tree . . . not engine detail shots.*

quality instant camera. They are available, but you won't find them for twenty bucks at the local drug store.

Even though you can't see the results instantly, the versatility of a decent 35MM single lens reflex camera is tough to beat. The built-in metering systems of these cameras make them a breeze to use. You can take many more shots and still have less money tied up in film and processing costs than with the instants. The quality is such that you can have a good blowup made if you need to see high detail. For those shots of areas where color isn't important, consider black and white film in 36 exposure rolls, processed with a "contact" sheet (a single print of all the roll's exposures at negative size). For just a few dollars, you can build a several-hundred photo portfolio of your car.

Documenting your car's condition before work begins doesn't have to be limited to photography. You can and should make written notes and sketches. You can record your observations on a tape recorder. You can even video tape with voice overlay if you're so inclined. Just be sure to do something. It'll be time well spent.

It's also a good idea to obtain manufacturers' data on your automobile. The older the car, the tougher this can be. But if you own something like a Corvette, there is a tremendous amount of literature available. All the owner's manuals are available, as are shop manuals and many books devoted to specific areas of interest. Copies of factory assembly manuals, complete right down to the last screw, are available for many Corvette models. These manuals were prepared by Chevrolet Engineering to show assembly plant personnel how to put the Corvette together, and they are invaluable to an enthusiast for obvious reasons.

Material is harder to obtain for some other cars with less enthusiast interest. But you may be surprised at how much actually is available if you take the time to look. The more data you can locate for your car, the better. Add it to the photographs and other materials you've compiled, and you're off to an excellent documentation start.

Once you've gotten the documentation business done to your satisfaction, you may be ready to start detailing. Then again, you may not be. The determining factor is the mechanical condition of your car. There's no point in detailing an engine compartment if old gaskets are allowing oil and fuel to dribble and seep out, or if the cylinder head is coming off soon for a valve job. There just isn't much of a mechanical nature you can do without fouling up a nicely detailed car at least a little. Plan to get every bit of the mechanical work you discover has to be done out of the way before you even start to think about cosmetics.

The order in which you do things is important. Once you've gotten the things of a repair nature finished, it's best to start with the engine and chassis work. It's this work that's most likely to foul the exterior and interior, so you definitely leave exterior and interior until last. You'll get differences of opinion on where the interior should be slotted in, and you can do as you see fit. We prefer doing the interior before the exterior, but there's nothing sacred about the order provided you've gotten the engine and chassis work out of the way before either the exterior or interior work starts.

Chapter Two

Engine and Chassis Detailing

A lot of people new to the art of detailing cars make the mistake of thinking they need a lot of equipment. They figure that to do it right they'll need a steam cleaner, a sandblaster, a glass beading cabinet, and a drum of eat-anything acid. All of these things come in handy at times, but they all share a common fault. They're destructive. They'll remove what you want to remove, and more. In severe cases, there will be no choice in the matter. You'll be forced to use whatever technique is required to get the surface in question back to where it can be refurbished. But many times a very conventional cleaning technique will bring the absolute worst looking engine compartment back to life. This is because the worst looking engine compartments are the ones that look like everything has been dunked in oily goo. Yet that oily goo may have been the perfect preservative for the paint, labels, decals, and codes below. It's the dry engine that looks like it has been sanded raw and left in a field to rust that is going to require the harsh and abrasive cleaning techniques.

Start your cleaning with some hot water, a variety of bristle brushes, an old washcloth, and a good grease dissolving dishwashing detergent like *Dawn*. Squirt the detergent on full strength and go to work with your washcloth and brushes. The detergent will eat the grease and oil off like magic (a few applications will be necessary on heavy buildups) but the surface under it will be unharmed. If you uncover a paper label, be careful not to brush it or the lettering and the label itself could be damaged. Keep a garden hose handy for rinsing. You can attack all engine compartment and chassis parts with this technique. It sounds like it would take forever, but it really doesn't. If you weren't planning a full fledged detailing job, but just wanted to get your everyday driver looking better, you'll likely be satisfied with the good detergent cleaning just described, followed with a few simple preservative tricks for some of the parts subject to deterioration.

There are nice advantages to the detergent technique over steaming, spray degreasers, or lacquer thinner type cleaning. The preservation of what's underneath the crud has already been mentioned. The preservation of your hands is another. Solvents like lacquer thinner are effective because they dissolve about everything . . . including your skin and the rubber gloves you bought to try to protect your skin. Don't take this to mean that you should throw your lacquer thinner out. It's one those things that will definitely be used somewhere during detailing. It just works so well for some tasks that it tends to get used at times when something milder will work just as well.

Of course, there are times when the detergent technique isn't applicable. Maybe your car's engine compartment has already been "detailed" by an amateur and all the original factory markings are gone anyway. Or maybe everything is gone because of old age. Or perhaps this pure factory originality business just isn't your bag and you want an engine that looks ten times better than anything that ever rolled out of the factory.

In these cases you can go with the standard practice of commercial steam cleaning, or the do-it-yourself variety. If you want to handle it yourself, buy a couple of engine degreasing spray bombs (*GUNK* is the best known) and head for the local self-serve spray wand car wash. While you're waiting in line, spray down the engine with the degreaser and let it soak in a while. (It works best on a hot engine). Then just hose it down. You may need a couple of applications, and you might want to help it along by doing some brushing during the soak cycles. Be prepared for some difficulty in restarting the engine. It's a good idea to bring along some soft, absorbent rags to dry out things like the inside of the distributor. You can mask off the electrical components to shield them from the water, or you can let the engine run during spraying (keep your hands clear!). If it starts to stumble, back off until it recovers.

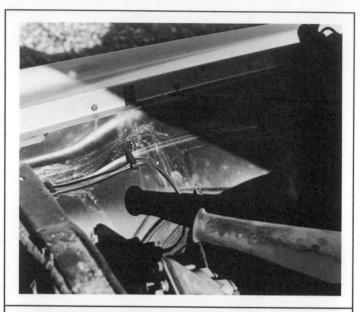

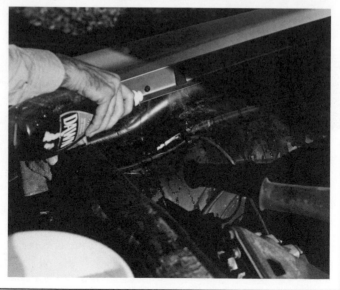

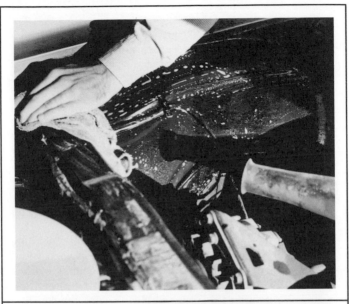

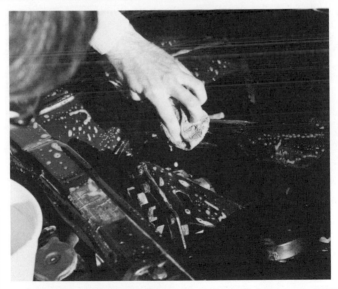

One problem with engine degreasers is that they smell. It's not necessarily a bad smell, but it's there and it will be there for a while. It bothers some people enough to prevent them from using this cleaning technique.

Now that everything is clean, make another mechanical component check and fix anything needing repairs before starting to detail. Be sure to check all the rubber hoses. They tend to deteriorate from the inside out, so an external visual check won't be conclusive, but you can get a pretty good idea by looking at the ends. If you replace a hose, don't just remove the clamp and start yanking. The correct procedure is to carefully split the end of the hose with a sharp knife or single edge razor blade, then peel the hose off. Lubricate the inside of the new hose with a bit of soap so it will slip on easily.

If up to this point you hadn't completely decided how extensively you want to detail, now's the time. You may find that your clean engine looks so good that nothing more is required. Or you may wish to go the full show car route. That will require considerable disassembly of engine components.

You have to also decide what type of detailing you want. If you lean to the cosmetic attractiveness of a show car, you'll want to disassemble and refinish components individually, then carefully reassemble. You may choose to enhance some components by upgrading their finishes. For instance, a raw steel fuel line could be chrome plated. Brass or aluminum parts could be polished to perfection.

On the other hand, you may lean to taking your car back to an "as built" condition. This would require some different tactics. You might disassemble and clean the components as before, but they shouldn't necessarily be individually refinished before replacing them. For example, Corvette engines with painted valve covers were nearly always painted

---

Pages 14-15: These photos show the progression from a typically grimy inner fender well, radiator top, and air cleaner snorkle through initial cleaning with dishwashing detergent and washcloth. Page 17: Above, cleaned area is rinsed with plain water. Results of twenty minutes of non-destructive cleaning effort is apparent below.

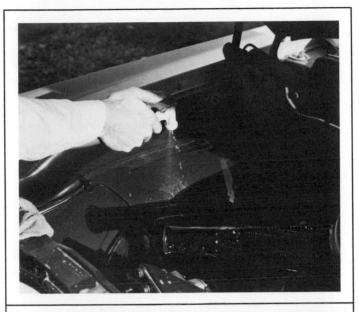

17

at the factory with the valve covers in place, as well as other components. This means that the edges of the valve cover gaskets would be painted. A show car would always have the valve covers finished separately and the gasket edges would not be painted. It just looks neater. But it won't look that way on an original car or one that's brought back to original condition. And of course when original factory look is the goal, the finish of any component is never enhanced or improved beyond what was typical of factory production.

Now to some specific refinish techniques. Engine surfaces should be repainted in an original type engine enamel. If yours is a relatively late model product of an American manufacturer, engine enamel spray bombs are readily available at any number of local sources. If your car is older, you may have to purchase from a specialized supplier. Any issue of *Hemmings Motor News* or *Cars & Parts* will yield several sources. You might also consider joining a marque club servicing your model that has some sort of periodical newsletter or magazine containing paint and part suppliers.

Don't use flat black enamel of the hardware store variety to respray the inner fender wells or black chassis components. It looks nice when you spray it, but it mars every time it's touched. Special chassis black paints are available which have just the right gloss and durability. These are also available in spray bombs or bulk from several sources, including GM dealers and auto paint stores. The drawback to a real chassis paint is that it's petroleum-based. That means a gas leak will eat it right off.

If you want to put a show car look on the chassis black areas under the engine compartment whether or not you've refinished them, try coating them with a product like *Armor All* or STP's *Son of a Gun*. These products are usually thought of as being limited to vinyls, rubbers, or leathers, but they are also effective on painted surfaces if a damp, satin look is desired. Show car people use this type of product in many more places than the ads recommend. When used in an engine compartment though, it has to be kept after. The heat from the engine will cause it to precipitate slightly and it must be wiped often. Wiping it just before judging creates a pristine look for the judge, but in a car that's being driven daily, the effect will soon be gone.

The best way to handle engine compartment chrome and brightwork is to remove it and clean it by hand in the sink using dishwater detergent and possibly a fine grade of steel wool. Once cleaned, apply several coats of good paste wax. Engine compartments are harsh environments for plated surfaces, so these have to be attended to regularly to maintain their attractiveness.

If the plating is gone off something like a fuel line, it has to be replated or replaced. Don Williams has found nearly perfect replacements in the plumbing supply section of a local hardware . . . toilet feed lines.

Wiring, including wiring harnesses, will usually come clean with the detergent treatment. If not, try gently brushing with lacquer thinner. Don't soak with lacquer thinner as the wire insulation coating or harness wrapping could be permanently damaged. Just brush it on lightly such that the stains are removed and the thinner evaporates quickly. Come back with the *Dawn* detergent bath once more, then coat with *Armor All* full strength. Let it soak for a few hours, then wipe with a soft cloth. You'll be amazed.

Don't soak with lacquer thinner as the wire insulation coating could be permanently damaged.

Instead of using lacquer thinner, Don Williams recommends trying Ditzler's *Acryli-Clean #DX330* first. This is a product made to clean surfaces prior to painting, but Don says he uses it a lot in the engine compartment because it is a tremendous cleaner and it doesn't eat into everything the way lacquer thinner does.

If rubber hoses don't need to be replaced, they can be made to look like new using the same technique just described for the wiring. But there are two cautions. First, if the hoses are the original factory type with printed codes, the lacquer thinner might wipe the codes off. There goes a little

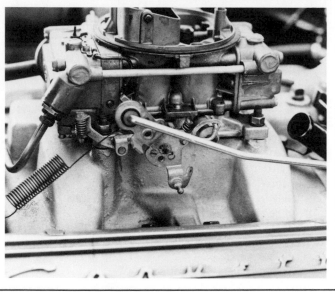

authenticity. Second, while lacquer thinner is a great cleaner, it's not a preservative. If anything, it will accelerate deterioration. But it does get the dirt and glaze off, allowing a preservative to get in and do its job. Follow a lacquer thinner treatment of rubber with *Armor All,* or a regular rubber preservative. The same stuff many gas stations use to lube a new tire bead before mounting is available in convenient pint or quart cans.

Thanks to leaky carburetors, intake manifolds always seem to need attention. For aluminum intakes, caution is necessary in the cleaning stage. Glass beading or sandblasting will definitely clean the surface, but it will also change the surface texture. Instead, try soaking in paint stripper. Gas stains, grease, and paint overspray will be gobbled up, but the aluminum will not be affected. Use a non-metallic bristle brush to work the stubborn stains and flush with water. For later maintenance of a little gas stain, direct a squirt of disc brake cleaner at the stain with one of the readily available spray bombs, and sop up with a paper towel. A squirt of carburetor cleaner will also work great.

A cast iron intake will probably have some rust and the paint stripper won't be adequate. Here the sandblast, glass bead, or acid-dip technique is acceptable as the underlying surface won't be affected much. If you go one of these routes, be sure to thoroughly clean the manifold afterward with compressed air, a good lacquer thinner scrub, and a super hot detergent bath. A mistake many detailers make is not getting all the little embedded particles of sand, glass, or acid residue out. Eventually this stuff can work its way out and take some paint along. Or worse, something left behind on the inside of an intake manifold can work loose and get carried into the inner workings of the engine.

There is a technique described in the following section for refinishing cast iron exhaust manifolds used by Dave Burroughs that will also work on cast iron intake manifolds.

Above Left: Fuel stains from leaking carburetors are common to intake manifolds. Direct a stream of carburetor or disc brake cleaner against the stain with spray container.
Below: After patting with paper towel, manifold is spotless.

Regardless of how you choose to get there, be sure the metal is clean and completely free of rust and cleaning debris before refinishing. The special enamel used on engine blocks works well on cast iron intake manifolds, and that's usually what the factory used originally.

As a side note, Don Williams blocks off the crossover passage on the Chevy manifolds of his show cars. The purpose of the crossover is to route some hot air under the carb to heat it, but the paint over that portion of the intake tends to discolor. Block the crossover and the intake looks like new indefinitely.

On the average engine, the worst looking components will invariably be the exhaust manifolds. In the case of older Corvettes and most other cars, the factory just sprays the manifolds with the same enamel as the rest of the engine. This paint has a higher temperature tolerance than the stuff you spray the lawn chairs with, but not nearly high enough to handle the scorching temperatures of the engine exhaust. After a couple of good highway drives, the paint is fried off or discolored severely.

The most common method of cleaning exhaust manifolds is by acid-dip, glass-beading or sandblasting, all acceptable. You can also wire brush them yourself if you don't have the other equipment. A bench-mounted wire brush attachment on a grinder works best as you can move the manifold across the brush face. You can also mount the manifold in a vise and attack it with a hand-held electric wire brush, or with an attachment in an electric drill. If you have the patience and time, there's also the old "armstrong" method. Follow the wire brushing with an *SOS* and hot water cleaning.

Once the exhaust manifolds are cleaned, there's a choice of several coating options. If you want them to look good with very little further effort, they can be porcelainized in a variety of colors, or chromed. If you're a stickler for origin-

---

Above Right: *The first step in the do-it-yourself technique for refurbishing an exhaust manifold for show car effect is wire brushing.*
Below Right: *After wire brushing, the manifold should be given a thorough cleaning in lacquer thinner.*

Above: Follow the lacquer thinner bath with SOS and hot water.
Right: While the manifold is still hot from the SOS bath, coat it generously with Armor All and let it soak well before buffing excess.

ality, you can just repaint them in engine enamel as the factory did. The paint will burn off, but if the car is used strictly for show and is started just for judges and short drives, they'll look decent and authentic for quite a while. There are also ultra-high temperature paints specifically for exhaust applications which work pretty well. They don't have the look of originality nor the durability of chroming or porcelainizing, but the price is right. Bill Munzer uses *VHT #SP102,* a 1350° flat black paint. He says it dries with no gloss, looks almost like a raw casting, and lasts quite a while.

If you're purely into show cars, here's another option. After sandblasting, glass beading, or wire brushing, give the manifold a scrub bath in extremely hot water and *SOS* as before. Let the manifolds air dry (it will take just a few seconds) then drench while still warm with *Armor All*. Let it

soak for a day. Then install and "burn in" by letting the engine warm up. The *Armor All* will bead up and dance on the manifold surface. Apply more to the hot manifold and continue doing so until it starts to absorb. Let the engine cool and wipe off the excess. You won't believe the results. The manifold will look like a virgin raw casting, but without any discoloration or rust. Plus, it will have a nice sheen to it. There's just one catch . . . it doesn't last. The beads will appear to some extent whenever the manifolds get hot, and the whole process has to be repeated to stay fresh. It's not practical at all for a street driven car. But for show effect, it's hard to beat. Don Williams has heard of people achieving similar results by using a mixture of graphite and motor oil.

Another trick that circulates among show car preparers is that of coating the inside surfaces of an exhaust manifold with oil before reinstalling. This is said to prevent a manifold that has been chromed from quickly turning blue.

Chapter Three

Interior Detailing

Painted interior surfaces usually aren't subjected to extreme wear and often can be cleaned well with a scented household cleaner. If surfaces are damaged such that refinishing is required, remove the pieces from the interior if at all possible. Do not try to match interior paint at the local hardware store. Many exact duplicates or acceptable matches can still be mixed by your local auto paint store. This will require spraying equipment, but the results will be worth it.

Vinyl interior components can be cleaned with a variety of products made specifically for the purpose. A product that a lot of show car people like to use for interior vinyl and other surfaces is a pump spray furniture polish like *Pledge*. An application of *Pledge* leaves a nicely protected finish with some gloss, but without the wet look of an *Armor All* type product. Lemon scented *Pledge* is popular because of the pleasant odor it leaves, though Bill Munzer reports he has had minor streaking problems with the lemon variety, and he prefers standard *Pledge* for interior vinyl.

Leather requires considerable additional care. Leather dries out and the moisture has to be replenished. But maintaining too much moisture can rot the stitching. Visit your local leather or saddle shop for a quality leather cleaner and a preservative containing neatsfoot oil. Let the oil compound soak in well and follow with a thorough buffing.

If leather is damaged, you may be able to refurbish it to an acceptable condition without replacing. If the surface has deteriorated but there are not splits or tears through the leather, it can be lightly sanded with 600 grit sandpaper to reveal a smooth, uncoated surface. Follow this with a spray or brush-on leather dye. A leather dye, such as *Ram-Cote*, is flexible and quite durable.

If a portion of the leather has simply lost its color due to light abrasion, such as an entry area of a seat, the color can

be replenished with paste shoe polish. You have to be careful to completely buff out all excess polish, otherwise it will transfer to your clothing. Follow with an application of a neatsfoot oil compound and buff again. Avoid using the shoe polish technique on a large seating area, because it is virtually impossible to prevent some of it from later transferring to clothing. The first time a sweet young thing hops into your newly redone black interior in a spotless white dress, you're going to be in big trouble.

There are some excellent household products available for cleaning your auto carpet. The best type to use is a spray foam that is applied directly to the carpet, worked in, and allowed to dry. When dry, the remaining residue is vacuumed out and the dirt comes with it. If your carpet is the closed loop kind, be careful what type of brush and brushing technique you use to work in the foam cleaner. The potential problem is that the brush can tear some fibers loose and your carpet winds up with the fuzzies. You may find it best to work the cleaner in with your hands, a rag, or a sponge.

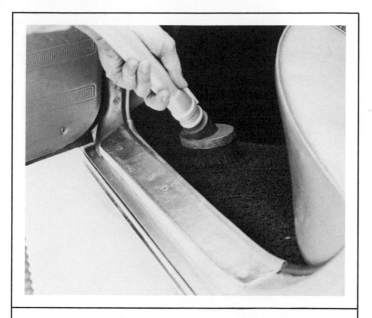

So long as there is no excessive wear or tears, you can nearly always bring carpet back to life. If there is a small isolated wear spot, such as an area a previous owner liked to rest a heel, you could try stealing a little carpet from under the seat and patching.

There are excellent spray dyes available to renew carpet color. One is called *Fabspray*. You should never attempt to change a carpet's color, only to renew it. The problem with a spray product is that color selection is limited. Black is black and you can spray dye a black carpet back to perfection. Any other color is going to be a problem. When using a spray product, work it into the carpet fibers with a lintless rag or sponge before it dries. If you don't, it tends to leave a sort of hard crust on top of the fibers. Rub it in and it will look better than new, even in moderately worn areas.

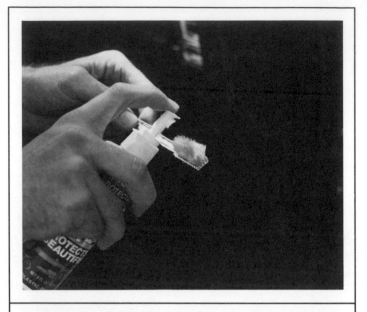

Above: It's often best to spray cleaner or protectant directly onto rag or brush because overspray may land where it's not wanted.
Right: Small brush sprayed with silicone protectant product is an effective method for removing dried wax residue from inside doors.

Dave Burroughs has good success mixing his own carpet dye using a household product like *Rit*. Other restorers have even dusted carpets with lacquer color coats successfully. Regardless of the technique you choose, be sure the carpet and its backing is absolutely dry before starting.

Interior rubber, such as door and glass seals, can be made to look like new with a little effort. Try cleaning with detergent first, but if that doesn't work, lacquer thinner will. Exercise extreme care using lacquer thinner because a stray dribble will eat everything in its way. It's best to carefully dampen a small area of a rag and work small areas of the rubber. Once the rubber is clean, apply a rubber lubricant or *Armor All*. If you find that the *Armor All* gives a more glossy appearance than desired, you're probably not buffing it out

adequately. Also, try thinning it with 50% water. (You seldom need to use it full strength.) This technique also works great on windshield wipers. They not only look great, but the softening effect makes them work like new.

Did you ever notice how the glass on a show car seems to sparkle? There are several ways to achieve it. Most show car people have a pump spray bottle of *Windex*, the type with

---

Did you ever notice how the glass on a show car seems to sparkle?

---

ammonia added, in their secret bag of tricks. Nothing secret about that, but the key is how it's applied. Contrary to the instructions, show car people find that *Windex* works best as a polish, not as a cleaner. In other words, you get the glass clean first, then polish it with the *Windex*. The mistake many people make is trying to clean an interior glass area with a few squirts of cleaner on a rag. The dirt just gets moved around. You must use liberal amounts of water to flush glass clean. You can combine that with a packaged glass cleaner if you wish, but a dab of ammonia or even kerosine works just as well. Once it's clean, then polish with *Windex*. There is a caution to using ammonia or ammonia-based products. They can stain paint a bit, especially the flat finish found on some painted dashboards. Exercise special care around painted surfaces. You may even wish to mask.

Another glass trick you may have heard about is the old newspaper routine. It's hard to believe that a newspaper, with that never-drying ink that gets all over your hands and white shirt, could actually be an effective window cleaner. It can be, but again only when used to polish clean glass. It's not the paper that does the trick, but the newspaper ink which acts as a very fine polishing abrasive.

Interior brightwork isn't subjected to the elements, and show car people often prefer not to wax it and have to worry about wax residue on adjacent surfaces. Instead, they just use *Windex* or a clear silicone product. Cleaning around little bezels, radio knobs, and other fine detail work is best accomplished with a mild dishwasher detergent, toothbrushes, and *Q-tips*.

Normally, you don't have to worry about instrument faces, but the clear glass or plastic lens will need cleaning or buffing. Clean glass as previously described. If the problem is on the inside surface, the instruments will have to be disassembled. After cleaning the inside of the glass, wipe it with a rag sprayed with *Endust*. This product actually makes the lint and dust adhere to the rag rather than vice versa. The same holds true for plastic lenses, but plastic may require some additional steps to get it crystal clear.

If plastic is scratched or cloudy, it can be brought back. The key is to remove the damage with a fine abrasive, then proceed through a series of finer abrasives until the surface is clear again. There are kits available to do this, such as one sold by Bobby Colvin as described in the following section in a discussion for removing scratches from convertible top windows. For plastic instrument lenses and other plastic parts, you can achieve excellent results by wet sanding with 600 grit sandpaper, then polishing with jeweler's rouge on a soft buffing wheel, or hand polishing with rouge. If you find that you can't remove the scratches left by the 600 grit, there are intermediate steps that will help. You can make your own 1000 grit or so sandpaper by rubbing two pieces of 600 together. Be sure to use it wet and be sure the scratches you're leaving for the next step are uniform. If there are scratches left over from a previous step (maybe you had to start with 400 grit), the jeweler's rouge will not likely remove them. Jeweler's rouge is as fine an abrasive as you're likely to need for auto polishing applications, but there is another excellent polish found in every home that is just slightly more abrasive than the rouge and is often adequate by itself or as a preliminary to the rouge. What is this magic substance? Toothpaste.

The procedures just described should only be used for seriously scratched or damaged surfaces. Always start with the mildest polishing technique and work into the more abrasive ones only if necessary. For plastic windows, both hard

and soft, John Amgwert has found that *MeGuiars* sealer
works incredibly well. John says he acquired a '54 Corvette
once with a convertible top window so bad he was sure it
would have to be replaced. After using *MeGuiars* sealer, the
window was so clear it looked like it had been removed.
Don't expect to do this in ten minutes though. Be prepared to
spend some time. And never work a flexible piece of plastic
if it's very hot or cold. When hot, the plastic stretches. When
cold, it breaks.

Don't attempt to refinish the actual face of an instrument
yourself. There are companies which offer this service, and
it's best left to them or not done at all. There seem to be a
lot more cases of people dissatisfied with instrument face
refurbishing than those delighted. Unless your instrument
faces are really bad, consider leaving them alone. Hand-held
air bombs sold in photo stores for dusting off negatives make
great instrument dusting devices. Hold these things perfectly
upright when using though, or they spit liquid freon prop-
ellant that could permanently stain the instrument face (or

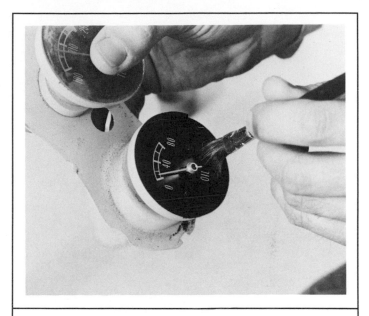

Left: Instruments and glass faces before cleaning.
Above: Soft camel hair brush is used to "dust" instrument face.
Page 36: Instrument glass is washed and polished (above), then carefully dusted with a rag sprayed with Endust (below).
Page 37: The difference between clean instrument below is apparent compared to untouched condition of instrument above.

blind you if the freon gets in your eyes.) Obviously, great care should be exercised around the instrument needles, and don't demagnetize the speedometer or cable-driven tachometer by poking your screwdriver in the wrong place.

Remove clutch and brake pedals completely from the car so you can work on them in the sink. Squeeze the rubber so that the grooves open and the fine particles can be brushed out. For a show car, soak the pedals in *Armor All* full strength, then polish. Make little cloth "footsies" to protect the pedals from foot scuffing when the car is being driven on and off a trailer. For a street driven car, the *Armor All* isn't a good idea because it makes pedals slippery. If you're not

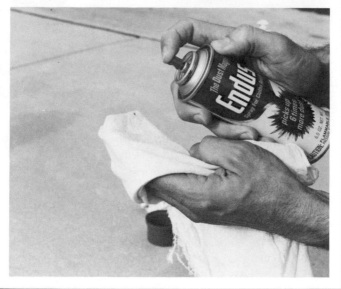

37

satisfied with the results of a good hot water dish detergent treatment, try a little lacquer thinner.

Technically speaking, products like *Armor All* and STP's *Son of a Gun* are considered by enthusiasts to be water-based compounds containing silicone. We phoned the manufacturers of *Armor All* to confirm the presence of silicone in their product, but they would neither affirm nor deny this. They prefer to call their product a water-base protectant and let it go at that.

As best we can determine, it is silicone that permits *Armor All* and products like it to work so effectively. But it should be pointed out that a good thing can be overdone. These products work so well for certain things that people tend to use them everywhere. There are places where their use may simply not be appropriate. John Amgwert reports that he regularly used a silicone product for the interior wood veneer trim panels of his '73 Corvette and promptly ruined the veneer. He's since seen '73 models with veneer that's never been touched and is still perfect.

Another contributor, Mike Antonick, reports that he used *Armor All* on the interior vinyl door panels and seats of a Corvette before putting it into storage for the winter. The surfaces treated developed a surface mold. Other untreated cars were in the same garage and had no problem. And the car that did develop the mold had been stored in the same garage the previous seven winters without being treated and without a problem.

We phoned the manufacturers of *Armor All* to ask if their product could encourage mold or mildew. They said absolutely not, **if it was used properly.** They pointed out that *Armor All* is water-based and that the instructions clearly specify that the excess be buffed out. If you don't buff the excess out, excess moisture will be left on the surface, and that will indeed invite mold growth. In the case of water-based protectants, don't make the mistake of assuming that more is better. Don't assume that if a little works great, a lot will work wonders. Use these products the way the people who make them advise. And give some thought to what you're covering and when. The products are great for preventing dryness. But if you're storing where humidity is high, they may work against you.

Also remember that silicone products make surfaces slippery. Usually that's great, because friction and wear are minimized. But if you like to put a radar detector on your

---

> *If you don't buff the excess out, excess surface moisture could invite mold growth.*

---

dash and temporarily hold it in place with a couple of loops of masking tape, the unit will be in your lap on the first turn. Nothing sticks to a dash treated with silicone.

Dave Burroughs has a nice trick for cleaning soiled seat belts. Since it's more a matter of soil being trapped between tightly woven fibers than actually being absorbed by the fibers, Dave removes the belts, lays them out, and blasts them with the high pressure wand at the do-it-yourself car wash. If the soil is really stubborn, try first working in some liquid dishwashing detergent by hand. Don Williams cleans his belts with *Ditzler DX330* cleaner and a fingernail brush.

Is there any reason not to clean seat belts? Could be. Some belts carry a warning against trying to wash them. Apparently there is a danger of the stitching rotting and the belt's safety being affected. John Amgwert suggests dry cleaning as a possibility to consider. Obviously, replacing the belts with brand new ones is the best bet. Any cleaning technique should be well thought out and based on the intended use of the car, among other considerations.

The first thing you see when you open a car door is the end of the door and the door jamb, both of which tend to accumulate dirt and seeping grease. Here's another area where something like *Dawn* dishwashing detergent works well. Put it on full strength and work around the rubber seals and the hinge/latch mechanisms with a toothbrush and your fingers. Rinse with plenty of warm water. If the rubber seals still look shabby, spruce them up with a rag moistened with lacquer thinner. Be careful not to rub the adjacent painted areas.

Above: Dishwashing detergent is used full strength on inner door.
Right: Grease is worked loose using detergent and fingers.
Page 42 Above: Bristle brush is effective for scrubbing around seals.
Page 42 Below: Damp towel is best for removing remaining residue and to bring surfaces to semi-dry state.
Page 43 Above: Armor All protectant is sprayed onto clean rubber seal. Test small area first to be sure protectant does not spot adjacent surfaces.
Page 43 Below: Don't forget rubber window seals. Apply rubber protectant to keep clean and soft. This prevents cracking, promotes a better seal, and minimizes window rattle and noise.
Page 44: Resulting door jamb and seals after clean-up. No disassembly was required.

Relubricate the lock and latch mechanisms with one of the products made for the purpose, but don't be overly generous. The lubricant attracts dirt. Go back over the rubber seals with a rubber lubricant or *Armor All*. Rub the excess off, and don't forget the rubber door glass seals.

Armor All works well on rubber and vinyl floor mats too. Be sure they're clean first, and thin the *Armor All* 50% with

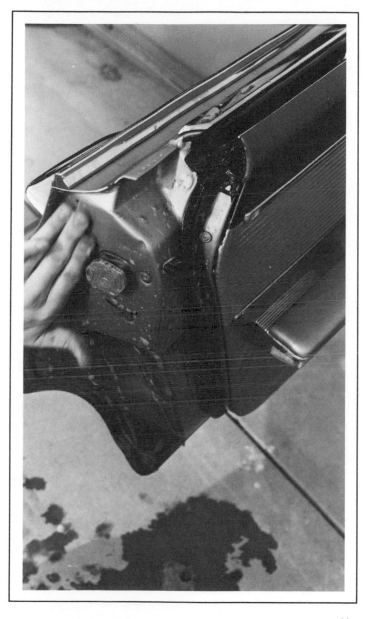

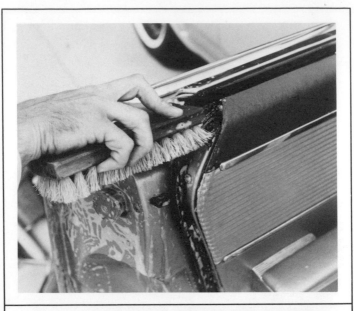

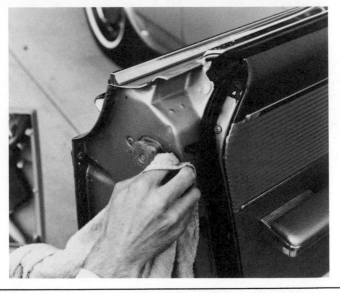

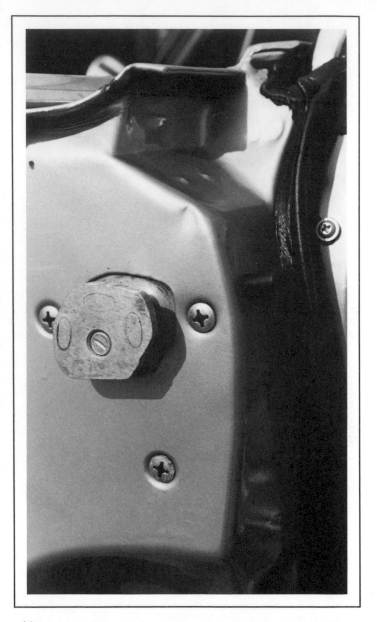

water. Do only the sides that face up. If you do the under-sides, the mats will slip around constantly.

In a car with genuine wood interior components, treat as you would any fine wood product. Furniture polish works well and a lemon-scented one will leave a fresh smell. Avoid keeping veneers too moist or peeling will result.

Speaking of fresh smell, there are some show car tricks for that as well. Once you've completed your interior cleaning, the scent should be pretty nice because most of the products mentioned are designed to leave a nice odor behind. You can enhance it even further with a Dave Burroughs technique.

First, he uses lemon-scented *Pledge* for nearly all of the interior hard surfaces. Then he leaves the *Pledge*-coated rags and a lemon scented air freshener inside the car with the windows rolled up tight for a week. Surprisingly, this doesn't leave a phony lemon scent. It's just a clean, fresh smell that lasts indefinitely. This isn't something you have to repeat every few weeks. Dave did it for his 1967 Corvette show car four years ago, and it still smells great inside.

Another trick used to keep an interior fresh in a car that's not being used daily is to leave an open box of baking soda inside. Better yet, dump the box into a pie pan for additional odor absorption. This is the old keep-the-refrigerator fresh trick, but it works for car interiors, too.

If your car already has a musty smell from damp storage, there is no single magic trick for getting it out. The interior should be dismantled as far as possible. Everything should be thoroughly cleaned, especially the carpeting which can really absorb and hold odors. In addition to the foam carpet cleaner mentioned earlier, there are dry types that you just shake into the carpet and vacuum. Corn starch will also work for this as well as baking soda. But test a section first. You need a strong vacuum and the carpet must be dry. After the interior cleaning, be sure to let the entire interior dry thor-oughly (nothing beats a hot, dry, breezy day) then follow with the Burroughs freshen-up with lemon *Pledge* and a lemon air freshener as just described.

Chapter Four

Exterior Detailing

No show car looks like a show car unless the exterior paint and brightwork gleam. Taking a car into the concours category almost always requires that the original paint be removed and the entire exterior professionally redone. It isn't within the scope of this text to get into that, but there are tricks and techniques that can be passed along that will enable you to bring an average finish back to near show car quality.

First, let's assume that the car in question has been street driven and has accumulated the usual road grime. The initial step is a squeaky clean washing. Start by coating the lower half of the car with kerosine, including the wheels, wheel covers, and tires. Excess rubbing isn't necessary or desirable. You'll scratch the surface. Just pat the kerosine on. It will soak out the speckles of tar and grit and they'll start streaking downward. Use liberal amounts of kerosine, and go through several applications until you're confident all the tar and other nasties have been soaked out. If your car has been undercoated, you'll have to exercise some care in this step because kerosine will thin petroleum-based undercoating materials.

Don't be concerned about the kerosine hurting your car's finish. It won't. Years ago, in fact, the old timers used to give their cars a kerosine soak periodically to keep rust from forming behind the chrome strips. And those expensive tar removers you buy are normally nothing more than kerosine with a little smell-good added.

If kerosine has a drawback, it is that it doesn't flush right off with clear water. Running the hose over it will take a lot off, but a film will remain. Dave Burroughs uses his old standby, *Dawn,* with warm water to wash kerosine off, but the products made specifically for washing cars, like

Dupont's powder car wash, also work fine. The key in this, or any car washing step, comes downs to this: Use liberal amounts of water, and be sure that the sponge or rag you are using isn't loaded with the grit you've just cleaned off.

If you see a guy washing a car in the early evening with a pile of rags or towels, constantly changing to a fresh washing surface, you can bet he knows what he's doing. If you see a small household sponge being used, the opposite is probably true. The biggest mistake people make cleaning a car is that they scratch the surface with the very grit they're removing. The scratches may be so small that individually they won't be noticed, but collectively they dull the surface. Obviously, on the first spring cleanup which is going to be followed by a rub-out and polish, this isn't as critical as when after the work has been completed, but it does add extra time. Don't ever take a car you care about through a car wash with the brushes that contact the car's surface. They claim that the brush material won't scratch an automotive finish. Maybe so, but the loads of dirt grit held by the brushes certainly will.

It's also a good idea to avoid washing a car in direct sunlight. The sun evaporates the water before it can be toweled off, leaving a residue that spots the paint, chrome and glass. Don Williams figures the drops act as magnifying glasses and burn the paint a little. In any event, the best time to wash a car is in the early evening when the sun is just going down.

Once you've got a clean, dry surface to work with, you can begin the process of bringing the finish back to life. The sequence of steps required to breathe new life into a really dead finish are: Fine sandpaper, rubbing compound, polish, and maybe wax. If there is any touch-up to be done, this is the time to do it. Also, if a panel or two had to be repainted, you can treat them as the rest of the body. In both cases though, it may not be necessary to go through all of the steps. A finish in decent shape may only need the polish step. One a little worse might require some selective rubbing compound treatment, followed by the polish. A poor original finish or a rough repaint may require the sanding step. Actually, many show cars do have all the steps despite near perfect paint application, but this takes some explaining. The rule for an existing finish is to do no more than required. Start with the lightest paint removal technique, polishing, and work a test patch to see if it's adequate. If not, go to rubbing compound. Only if the compound won't do the job, should you consider the sanding.

We're heavy on the cautions here because rubbing compound, and especially wet sanding, removes considerable amounts of paint. If your finish has been around a while, it may already be getting thin. A little sanding and rubbing, and the primer shows through.

A few years ago, Bill Munzer and Don Williams built a winning Corvette show car with a finish that approached perfection. *Corvette! The Sensuous American,* a hardbound Corvette periodical, carried a story of the restoration, and included a sidebar on the importance of sanding to achieve a show-car finish. We quote:

"Everyone knows that body refinishing requires a great deal of sanding. What many people don't know is that the most important step of all is the last one, the sanding of the final topcoat.

"You'll have to search a long way to find a body shop which sands the final topcoat before polishing. They'll look at you like you're half crazy if you request it. The argument you'll get is that sanding removes too much paint. The real reason is that too much time is required.

"Bill Munzer's and most winning show cars have had this last crucial sanding step. Regardless of how well the final paint coat is applied, there will exist some small degree of texturing in the paint surface—think of it as a series of microscopic peaks and valleys. When polishing by hand or even a power buffer, the peaks are smoothed down, but the valleys get deepened a little at the same time. This is due to the flexibility of the polishing cloth or buffer pad. No matter how long you polish, the surface will never be dead flat.

"By wet sanding first with well-worn 600 grit sandpaper, backed with a hard rubber block, the surface can be trued before polishing.

"The one word of caution is that sanding does indeed

remove paint and this must be done with extreme care. As the surface is being sanded, the portions touched by the paper will take on a dull sheen. The untouched low spots will stay bright and shiny. It's a good idea to leave just a trace of the shiny specs as a depth guide. If you sand until nothing is left but the sheen, you may go too deep.

"Work slowly and work small areas. Who knows, your efforts might win you a new Corvette one of these days."

There were a few things covered elsewhere in the Munzer article that bear on the sanding technique. Most important is the fact that when Don Williams sprayed the color coats on the car, he put double coats on all the character lines and peaks. This is because as you're sanding and polishing, these areas tend to get more attention. With a car that hasn't been so painted, you have to be extremely cautious not to sand or rub through these areas. In any event, use lots of water to keep the sandpaper clean. If you've got plenty of paint to work with, you can use a power buffer after the sanding step to get the bulk of the work done, then follow by hand to take the buffer marks out. But with an existing finish, using a power buffer is extremely dangerous. It almost has to be done by hand, and a hand-sand and polish of an entire car is very time consuming. These are all factors to consider before deciding what approach to take.

Remember too that the main purpose of the wet sanding is to smooth the finish to a dead flat surface. Skipping the sanding step won't result in a car with any less gloss, just with less of that perfect smoothness characteristic of a show car.

Another caution in the sanding step is that the paper has to be kept flat. This is accomplished by backing the paper with something other than fingers. Fingers cause uneven pressure and grooves. A hard rubber block is recommended, but there will be surfaces with curves that won't accept a rigid block. It may be necessary to use a sanding device with a flexible foam backing. John Amgwert wraps sandpaper around small sections of radiator hose, heater hose, etc. But let's face it, in some areas paper and fingers will be the only plausible technique. If so, minimize the grooving danger by folding the

Above: Toothpaste is an effective mild polish and cleaner, but remember that it is slightly abrasive.
Right: Try detergent bath first on emblems and use toothpaste where necessary to remove stubborn residue. Be cautious on painted surfaces.

sandpaper over a few times, and continually change the direction of sanding.

Rubbing compound follows the wet sanding. If you've skipped the sanding, rubbing compound will be the first step. Rubbing compound, especially hand applied, doesn't take paint off nearly as quickly as sanding, but it is a paint removal process and the same cautions apply. For cars just being freshened, it will be necessary to use the compound only in selected areas. Stubborn stains can be taken out with rubbing compound, as well as those scratched areas around door handles and locks. Something milder will usually get rid of dried bugs on the front-end surfaces, but if they've been there for a long period, they may have to be rubbed out with compound.

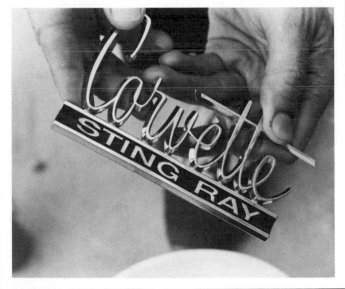

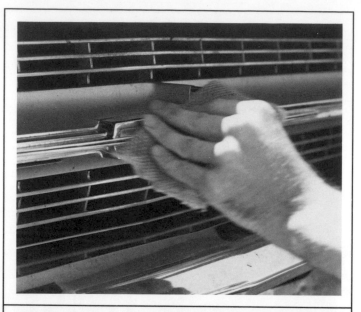

Above Left: Surfaces of emblems requiring repainting should first be thoroughly cleaned. Light sanding may be needed to smooth chips.
Below Left: Area to be painted is carefully masked.
Above: Allow for overspray if emblem has not been removed.

Buy your rubbing compound at an auto paint jobber. You'll have to buy a larger quantity, but you'll eventually use it and the price is much more reasonable. A favorite of show car people is *Dupont #606*, a fine white compound formulated specially for hand use. The compound should be thinned with water to a smooth paste consistency. Consider transferring some from the can to a squeeze bottle, pre-mixed with water.

Everyone develops the type of hand motion best suited for the finish being worked on. The important thing to remember with rubbing compound is to apply considerable pressure when first starting, then lighten as the compound starts to dry. You don't put compound on, let it dry, then remove like you do wax. Keep working the compound as it dries until it disappears. If you've lightened your pressure as the compound dries, the finished section will be bright and shiny. A little bit of compound will remain ground into the finish though, and some people like to give the car a washing before polishing.

Ask a dozen show car people what kind of polish they prefer, and you'll likely get eight or ten different answers. Dave Burroughs grew up around airplanes and the folks at the local airport like a product called *Astro-Shield* to keep their aircraft looking new. Dave has never found anything he likes better and still uses it for all his cars. It's a polish, but he finds that it protects so well that wax isn't necessary. He believes waxes tend to accumulate and yellow a bit. Not so with the *Astro-Shield*.

Walk through a concours event, and you're likely to see a number of other personal favorites. Products called *The Treatment* are common, as is *MeGuiars, Mother's,* and old faithful, *Dupont #7* polish. There are a raft of silicone based waxes and polishes on the market now and many offer incredible long-term protection. But they're designed to put on and forget . . . great for the salesman who wants a decent looking car without much trouble. Show car people want to

---

Many are not convinced the silicone products give the level of wet-looking gloss that they seek.

---

constantly keep after their car's exterior finish, and many are not convinced that the new products give the level of wet-looking gloss they seek.

Application technique for polish is important. Some products come with a little cloth-faced sponge for application. Fine for your knock-around car, not so fine for your pride and joy. No matter how thoroughly a car's exterior has been cleaned prior to polishing, some grit will remain. The reusable sponge jobbie will grab it and hold it, and fine scratching will be a certainty. If you're following a rubbing compound treatment, some of the compound grit will remain embedded

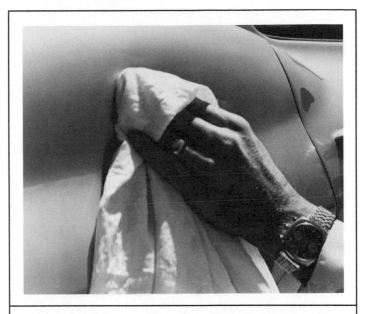

Above: This is an example of how not to polish a car. Do not use a crumpled up wad of rag. Parts of the rag will have no polish and can scratch the surface. Never wear rings or other jewelry while polishing a car, and take note also of zippers and belt buckles.

in the finish. The polish will lift it out and into your applicator.

The best bet is to use soft rags and plenty of them. Bill Munzer orders well used and laundered diapers from the local diaper service for the final polishing of his show cars. They're nearly lintless, and you'll find nothing softer other than maybe cotton balls. Bill uses those too. Right before judging, Bill puts a mist coat of *Windex* on all painted surfaces one area at a time, then wipes it down with a diaper. He says it leaves a beautiful shine with no lint. He uses a soft, pure bristle brush around emblems and body seams.

Dave Burroughs uses soft cotton rags and a two finger technique. The cloth is wrapped around two fingers, the polish applied and worked into a small area. Dave gets up close to what he's doing and goes slowly. He advises against pour-

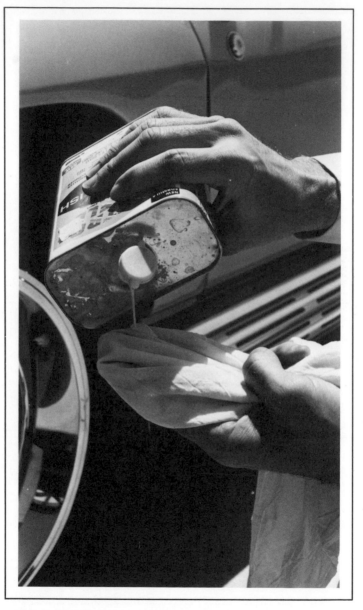

ing polish into a big wad of crumpled rag. Too much of the rag's surface won't have the polish.

Milt Antonick reports that in the model shop near his studio at Chrysler, there was a giant roll of cheesecloth. You just unrolled what you needed, and cut it off. Cheesecloth is expensive, but if you could locate it in bulk from an industrial supplier, a roll of it in the garage ala the Chrysler model shop would certainly come in handy.

Another tip from Bill Munzer: He thinks the best dusters in the world are made from ostrich feathers. He uses a big one to dust off his car just before judging. The word of caution is to watch out for little pieces of feather that get lodged behind corners of chrome, emblems, etc, that could possibly cause a points deduction.

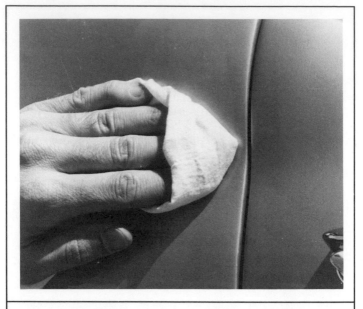

Above: One way to avoid polish and wax buildup along body seams, doors, etc., is to keep the polish or wax about a quarter-inch away from these areas. Your clean polishing rag will hold sufficient residue to shine the small strip later. This works only on a surface that is already in decent condition.

Nothing looks worse on a newly freshened car than globs of dried wax or polish in all the cracks and crevices. The first time a car is done, the necessary time will just have to be spent to polish these areas to get all the excess out. But once a car is done, there's no need to go through all this. When polish is applied, just keep the application a quarter-inch or so away from the cracks and crevices. When you buff out, there will be enough polish in your buffing rag to impart gloss to the small surface skipped. This technique will work on all but the most critical colors, such as black and dark metallics.

The common mistake made in the application of polish is a too generous dose. In polish application, more is not better. Heavy application leaves streaks and immediately clogs rags. Use sparingly and rub in well with moderate pressure, lightening pressure as the polish begins to dry. Properly done, the dried polish will hardly be visible, and will wisk off quickly with a clean rag.

The decision to wax is up to you. Most show car people don't, but then most of them don't expose their cars to the elements. If you want extra protection for the finish you've labored so hard on, there's nothing wrong with an application of fine carnauba-based wax. Paste is the longest-lasting, and a product like *Classic Car Wax* will give fine results, especially on a finish that's been previously groomed with the right rubbing and polishing steps.

Chrome exterior surfaces on a show car have to be perfect. If show is your goal, most likely the bumpers and other chrome trim will have to be removed and replated by a reputable firm, hopefully one specializing in auto restoration. To make chrome sparkle, Bill Munzer cleans with *Ditzler DX330,* washes, then shines with *Windex.*

If you just want to get what you have looking better, here are the steps to follow. First, try cleaning the chrome along with the body surfaces. Give it the kerosine bath treatment, then follow with polish to see if that will do the job. Don't use sandpaper or rubbing compound. Don't use regular steel wood pads either. If there are stubborn rusty areas, go after them with the finest grade of steel wool you can buy, dampened with an oil product like *WD-40* (Dave Burroughs prefers *G-96,* a favorite of gun collectors). Working a rust area the size of a dime might reveal that the source is a pin-hole size break in the chrome. Clean the oil off with a hot dishwashing detergent bath, then thoroughly dry and seal the breaks with a good carnauba paste wax. If the rust spot you

You won't win any shows with this stop-gap technique, but the chrome will look awfully good.

uncover is larger than pin-size, try dabbing a bit of high gloss aluminum paint on it before waxing. You won't win any shows with this stop-gap technique, but the chrome will look awfully good from a few steps away.

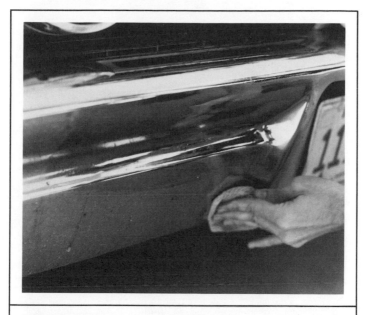

Left: *Even a bumper with rusty areas like this can be made to look almost like new with the right techniques.*
Above: *First, clean the bumper thoroughly using a nylon bug sponge.*
Page 62: *Apply a fine penetrating oil like G-96 or WD-40 to fine grade (0000 type) steel wool (above), then gently work the rusty areas of the chrome. Avoid using steel wool on chrome in good condition.*
Page 63: *After buffing out excess oil, apply several coats of a high quality wax. Apply thin coats or streaking will result.*
Page 64: *Results of final polish are evident. Note that the steel wool technique is for a bumper showing some rust from pin hole flaws. Avoid using steel wool on any exterior automotive surface unless absolutely necessary.*

Exterior glass cleaning techniques are much the same as described for the interior, except easier because it's more convenient to flush the glass with generous doses of water. One of the little nylon covered sponges made specifically for cleaning auto windshields works well for clearing away bugs and grime. Dish washing detergents have anti-spotting agents that help them flush clean. Once the grime is gone, the

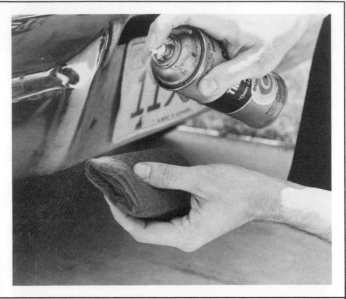

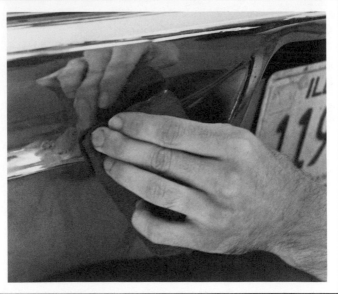

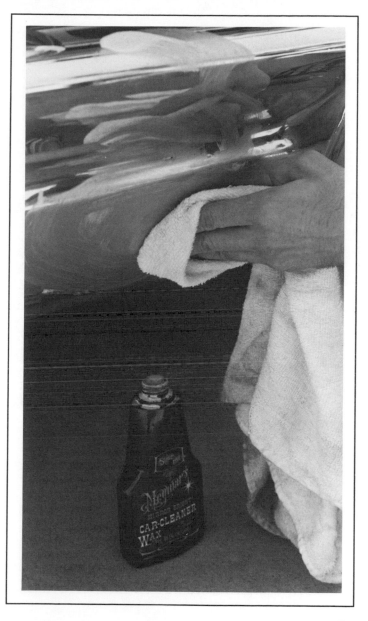

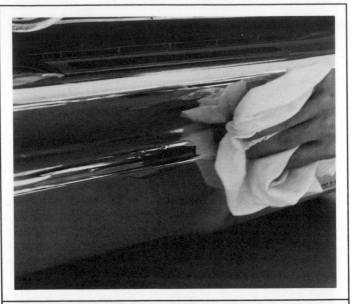

already-discussed techniques of polishing with *Windex* or newspaper can be employed.

Did you ever notice that after washing your car, the chrome and glass surfaces have to be wiped to prevent spotting, yet when you get into your car after a rain shower, the glass is clean and bright? The reason is the water itself. If a car is dirty and gets rained on, it looks lousy because the dirt gets collected in drops of rain water, then stays when the drops dry. But a clean car exposed to a shower often comes out looking great. If your car is stored inside, you might consider moving it out for a natural rain shower rinse, then move it back inside and towel it off. The glass will look especially nice. Some enthusiasts go so far as to keep some

---

Show car people don't use chamois because they streak and can also hold damaging dirt particles.

---

captured rain water handy for rinsing glass and chrome. If you don't like that idea, you can head for the corner drug store and buy a jug of distilled water. Water from a home softening unit also works. Regardless of your water source, don't chamois the finish off if you want the best results. A chamois kept well-rinsed will do a passable job on your everyday street machine, but show people don't use them because they streak and also hold potentially damaging dirt particles. Show car people usually like turkish towels and plenty of them.

Most people assume that a scratched or chipped windshield has to be replaced. Not necessarily. A good glass shop will have special compounds for polishing scratches out of glass. These require a lot of effort but they do work. In the case of a deep scratch, you may not be able to actually remove the scratch, but polishing the scratch will leave a clean groove that is hardly noticeable.

A chip in glass can be repaired by something called the *Novus* process. Only a handful of auto glass shops are equipped to do this, but it works like magic. The process

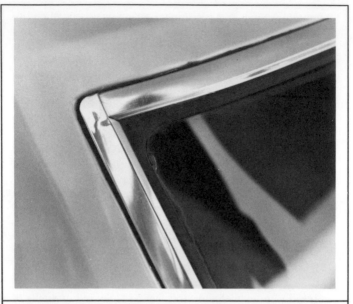

involves cleaning and polishing the cloudiness out, then filling the crack with an injection of a resin material. In the case of a typical stone chip resembling a spider web, the resin is put in under pressure such that the voids are filled. After it hardens, excess resin on the glass surface is polished. The result is not perfect, but it is extremely good. It is also relatively expensive. Fixing a chip costs roughly 25% of the cost of a new windshield. Logic would say that if you have more than a few chips, you might as well spring for a replacement windshield. True enough, except if your special car still has its original windshield, it might be nice to keep it in there for authenticity. Plus replacing a windshield often invites new problems. Chrome retaining strips get bent or scratched. Leaks are sometimes introduced. Look into getting your glass repaired before you make the final decision to replace it.

Here's one last glass tip from Dave Burroughs. One of those things that distinguishes show car glass from that of an average car is that the glass will be perfectly clean right up to the seal. Look closely at your own car and you're likely to see a little bit of crud on the glass right where it enters the seal. Over the years, that little layer of crud gets very hard and durable. To remove it, Dave Burroughs wraps a little very fine steel wool (0000 grade) around a small stick, squirts it with *Windex* or *Dawn,* and goes to work. The dirt comes off like magic. This is something you do gingerly, and you definitely don't go after glass with steel wool as a general rule. Use this technique delicately, and only for hard-to-reach stubborn areas along the glass edge. For easier areas to reach, a single edge razor blade can also be employed. Contrary to what you might have heard, both steel wool and a razor blade can damage glass, so proceed with care.

Plexiglas™, such as that in a convertible's rear window, is an entirely different ball game. Never put any steel surface

Above Left: On a neglected car, buildup of a hard crust along inner seals of glass is common. A mark of a show car is clean glass right to the seal.
Below Left: A handy method of cleaning a buildup along glass seal is to use 0000 grade steel wool on a stick dipped in Windex. Exercise care.

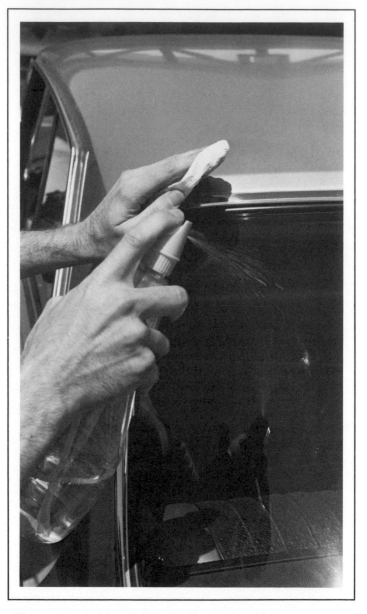

up to plexiglas. Don't even use the nylon-covered bug sponge. Plexiglas is soft. Its softness permits you to remove existing scratches, but allows new ones to be put in very easily.

The correct way to wash plexiglas is to thoroughly drench it with water before putting a washing cloth against it. Use an absolute minimum of pressure and just let the dirt float away with continual water flushing. Use a dabbing motion with your cleaning cloth, not a back and forth motion.

Both the rigid type plexiglas as found in an older Corvette's removable hardtop, and the flexible type found in many convertible tops, is prone to scratching and dulling with age, but both can be brought back. If the damage is minimal, you may get by with your favorite polish or wax. A wax like *Classic Car Wax* will remove fine scratches and leave the surface clear, shiny, and protected. John Amgwert says he's tried everything he can get his hands on, including some products made especially for the purpose, and nothing beats *MeGuiars* sealer for polishing plexiglas and plastic. But if scratches are really deep, you'll need to invest some time to get them out. So long as they're not extremely deep, they can be removed.

Removing scratches from plexiglas, or any plastic, is a matter of abrading the surface around the scratch down to the level of the bottom of the scratch, then removing the new scratches introduced by continuing to work the area with a graduated series of ever finer abrasives. The final abrasive is a fine polish, such as jeweler's rouge.

If you're serious about all this, you can invest in a kit of materials designed specifically for removing scratches from plexiglas. One is sold by a gentleman named Bobby Colvin, and contains spongy-backed abrasive pads of several grits and several bottles of special polishing and stain removing fluids. Dave Burroughs has this kit and says it works well.

Left: Spray glass cleaners are very effective for polishing glass that is already clean. However, some people find that the cleaners spot adjacent surfaces like window trim. If spraying directly onto the glass, develop a masking technique with the polish rag as shown.

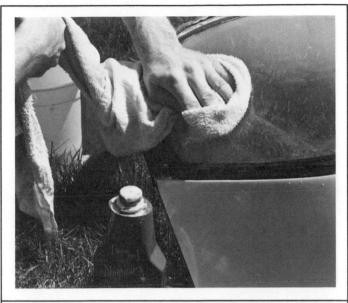

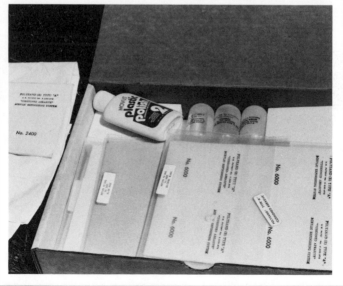

Pages 70 & 71: Always wash plexiglas by drenching in water first. Use polish or wax to remove fine scratches. Sand as a last resort.
Pages 72 & 73: Kits are available with graduated abrasive pads for removing deep scratches from plexiglas. They work well but require patience and time.

Some people put rubbing compound on plexiglas and go at it with a power buffer. To each his own, but this is risky business. Power buffing generates heat and heat can scorch plastic materials.

As is always the case, do some experimenting and use as fine an abrasive as you can to get the job done. On flexible plexiglas top windows, use a minimum of pressure. Otherwise, the plexiglas will stretch and you've got a puckered window. This is especially true if you're working on a warm day. Avoid cold days too, because flexible plexiglas gets stiff and may crack.

All of the techniques mentioned for plexiglas can also be used for other parts like taillight lenses and plastic trim. These parts have the additional advantage of being removable to be worked on a buffing wheel. Develop a very light touch on the buffing wheel to avoid the burning problem.

Another item that really stands out on a show car compared to a street car is the tires. The "average Joe" sorta figures that tires are like license plates . . . they're on the car but not really part of it. So tires get a light pass with the hose and that's it. Show car people know that spotless tires are a must for successful presentation. We're not talking about that awful tire paint stuff that used car dealers use. We're talking about a spotlessly clean tire with just the right sheen. It doesn't overpower the wheel or car body, but compliments it.

Here's Dave Burrough's procedure for making anything from old street rubber to off-the-shelf brand new tires look fantastic. Start with a scrub brush, a bucket of hot water, *Dawn* dishwashing detergent, and a hose. Rinse the tire down, then go after it with pure *Dawn* squirted directly onto the tire. Brush it in well then hose down and repeat until the grime is gone. If it's a whitewall, don't expect it to be spotless yet. Let dry, then squirt on a good whitewall bleaching cleaner. Dave uses one called *Sid Savage's Auto Cleaner,* mixed 50/50 with water. *Westley's* is probably the most popular and it works great too. Brush in using a tight, circular motion. Do the whole tire, not just the whitewall. Rinse thoroughly, repeat if necessary, and let the tire dry. If in a hurry, pat the tire dry. A word of caution when using tire bleach products. They can stain an aluminum or alloy wheel permanently. If your car has such wheels, don't risk using one of these products. If you're in doubt, either don't use a bleaching cleaner, or test a very small portion of your wheel to convince yourself it's safe.

Now saturate the tire with *Armor All* full strength. Let it soak in for at least a half hour . . . all day wouldn't hurt. If it doesn't stay wet, apply more. Finish the job by rinsing off the excess *Armor All* and polishing the tire with a dry towel. This technique will give the tire the semi-gloss show look. If you want the "dry" look, scrub the tire with *SOS* and warm water after the *Armor All* soak, then polish. Enough of the *Armor All* will have soaked in to give the tire the right look, but the *SOS* will impart a dull sheen. It'll look gorgeous

either way. And you'll be able to maintain it for quite a while by just washing with a mild cleaner. In fact, after Dave Burroughs has a car the way he wants it, he just uses a clear water wash in the evening with no soap whatever for the entire exterior.

One of the old-time tricks for making tires look good is brake fluid. It does work, but brake fluid is murder on paint and is very risky. With the products on the market today, there's just no reason to resort to it.

Wheels are another item that have to look good for overall show car effect. For a standard steel wheel and hubcap setup, clean the hubcap as you would any other exterior brightwork. Even though only a bit of wheel may be showing between the hubcap and tire, it is necessary to get it looking good. The ultimate way is to remove the tire from the wheel and strip the wheel to bare metal using paint stripper. Reprime and repaint the wheel in its original color. Usually enamel is the factory choice, even on cars with lacquer exterior finishes, because of enamel's superior durability and resistance to chipping. Also, it doesn't require buffing like lacquer.

Protect the rim from scuffing as much as possible when the tire is reinstalled. For real perfection, reinstall the tire, then break the outside sealing bead such that you can touch-up any scratches put on when the tire was installed, without slopping paint onto the tire itself.

The shortcut technique is to just work on the wheel with the tire mounted. The difficult part is masking the tire effec-

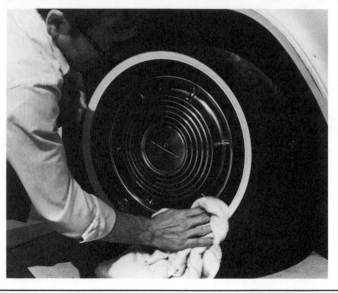

tively when repainting the rim, but a decent job can be done if you cut your masking tape every quarter-inch or so to permit it to bend into the desired rim curvature. Don't expect the tape to stick if you've already treated the tire with *Armor All*.

Our experts offer some other wheel painting ideas. Bill Munzer says if you don't want to break the tire bead, use quarter-inch masking tape to mask the tire and poke it behind the rim edge with a sharp object. Then use three-quarter-inch masking tape over the quarter-inch. Tuck newspaper under the outside edge of the wider masking tape. Bill further suggests removing the tape as soon as the paint is tacky so that it doesn't soak through the tape and onto the tire.

John Amgwert suggests breaking the tire bead but leaving the tire on and coating the tire with grease before painting the wheel. No masking is required as the paint won't stick to the greased tire. Just be careful not to slop any grease onto the rim, because the paint won't stick there either.

Milt Antonick doesn't break the tire bead, but makes his mask out of aluminum foil trimmed with a frisket knife. The

---

The aluminum foil conforms to the tire shape and will usually hold itself in place.

---

foil conforms to the tire shape and usually will hold itself in place. If not, dust the back of the mask with a spray adhesive of the type found in art stores.

If your car has wire wheels, cleaning and maintaining them is completely different from standard wheels. If they've been let go for awhile, they may need to be shipped back to the manufacturer, or to a company specializing in rebuilding wires; such as the *Dayton Wire Wheel Company*. What these people do is replace any damaged spokes, tighten all spokes and bring the wheel back to perfect true. Once the wheel is right, you can maintain it yourself pretty well by tightening loose spokes and replacing any that break. Eventually though, all wires have to get the full factory treatment.

If the wire wheels are painted, refurbishing them cosmetically involves the obvious steps of a thorough cleaning and a repaint. Painted wire wheels were popular on the British sports cars of the fifties and sixties. If you have one of these and the rear wheels get soiled by grease creeping out from the center hub, seal the area off with some silicone window caulk from the inside after you've cleaned them.

Chrome wire wheels are cleaned just like any other exterior chrome, it just takes a lot more effort. *Dayton Wire Wheel* manufactures new wire wheels for a number of contemporary applications, and they recommend periodically squirting *WD-40* onto all the spoke ends. This stuff is a great creeper, and prevents rust from making its way from the inside of the rim or around the nipples onto the spokes. The *WD-40* can be wiped and buffed just like a polish. Milt Antonick suggests buying products like *WD-40* in liquid bulk and transferring to old pump-spray Windex bottles as needed.

If your car has cast-aluminum wheels, such as the beautiful optional wheels available on 1963-1967 Corvettes, refurbishing techniques will be somewhat different. The Corvette wheels have fine detail fins and to get all the nooks and crannies clean, Dave Burroughs scrubs his in the bathtub and uses the shower head for a hot rinse. If the wheels have painted sections, special paints are available in spray bombs. Dave has always found that the original paint on any Corvette knock-off wheel in decent condition could be brought back by soaking it in *Armor All*. The fins and side rim can be refurbished using fine steel wool. If a nick has to be removed, it will have to be sanded with a series of wet/dry sandpapers, much as a scratch would be removed from plexiglas. On the fin faces of the 1963-1967 wheels, light machining marks are visible on original wheels and these can be

Page 81: Genuine aluminum or mag wheels like these beautiful mid-year Corvette wheels, can be refurbished using 600 grit sandpaper and fine oil like G-96 or WD-40. This duplicates the original machining marks of the wheel, but must be done slowly and cautiously.

Page 82: For a higher gloss, follow sanding with steel wool and polish.

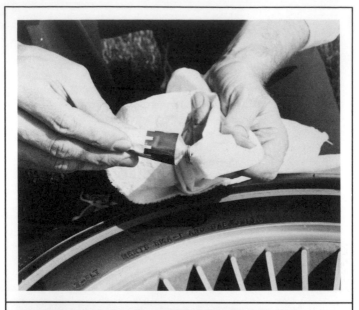

reproduced using 600 grit sandpaper with a light oil. A show car look would be achieved by following with steel wool and then polishing with a high gloss chrome polish, such as *Semi-Chrome,* or *Mother's Mag & Aluminum Jelly.*

One item on a street car that might not be able to be brought back to near show car condition is the convertible top. You can use the techniques covered earlier to spruce up the rear window, but some are beyond help. If the top material is still good, maybe a new rear window can be stitched in.

Convertible tops deteriorate because they're seldom properly cared for. Nothing is worse for a top than to be folded up dirty. The window gets scarred and the canvas gets scrunched against itself with abrasive dirt between. Start now by making it a practice never to fold a convertible top unless it's clean. If you have a convertible with a removable hardtop for winter use, take the convertible top out completely and store in an unfolded position.

Convertible top cleaners are available and they work as well as anything. If stains are persistent, try some of the products made for cleaning plastic bathroom showers and tubs, like *Soft Scrub* or Dow's *Bathroom Cleaner* with "scrubbing bubbles". These have good stain removing qualities without the harsh abrasives of standard kitchen cleaners. If you're at the point of giving up and buying a new top, you can resort to *SOS,* but this would be a once-only proposition. Steel wool is just too harsh for even occasional use.

Here's one more exterior trick from Don Williams, and it's a dandy. Don always has a black permanent *magic marker* in his show car kit. Nothing is handier for touching up tiny nicks on black chassis parts. Another place a marker can come in handy is on bright moldings such as those around windshields, that have been painted black by the factory. A tiny chip lets the silver metallic show through, but the marker will cover it beautifully, and it sticks. Don't go overboard with this idea. Marker ink looks a little blue against the blacks you'll be covering. This is strictly for small nicks.

Chapter Five

Maintenance and Storage

By now it's no secret that the way to get a car looking great is a knowledge of the right materials and techniques, and a lot of work. Having invested the time and money, it makes good sense to maintain your car in pristine condition. Once you go through the work of getting it there, keeping it there isn't too difficult. But you must understand that nothing you can do will preserve your car in the pristine condition it was when new, or even when refurbished. A car's condition deteriorates constantly.

In a sense, a car is like a human body. The analogy isn't perfect, because a car starts to deteriorate from the day it is made. Our bodies start to go downhill somewhere after maturity. Another hole in the analogy is that the process is basically irreversible for the body, despite the efforts of some of history's wealthiest people. An automobile can be brought back to near-new, but then the deterioration starts all over.

But the analogy holds in many ways. Proper care of our bodies can extend the quality and length of life appreciably. Care includes putting the right things in, the correct exposure to the elements, the right amount and type of exercise. The same holds true for an automobile. But there's a catch. Nothing is guaranteed. You can take perfect care of your body and check out twenty years ahead of your neighbor

who does all the wrong things. But take care of y[...]
the odds swing heavily in your favor.

With cars, there are a number of things that car[...]
slow the process of deterioration. But there is no assurance
that even with the proper care, deterioration won't be excessive. Besides that, there's always some disagreement over
what constitutes "proper" care anyway. It makes the most
sense to swing the odds in your favor and to do the right
things as best you can determine them.

Is there one single thing you can do to keep your very
special car in the best possible condition? Yes. Drive it! A
fifteen year old Corvette with five miles on the odometer
makes for an interesting story. But the truth is that the same
car with 15,000 miles on it, accumulated in weekly twenty
mile trips, would very likely be in much better condition.
There are things you can do if a car is being put into cold
storage for an extended period and we'll get to them in a
moment. But nothing beats giving a car regular exercise. Just
starting it up isn't adequate, nor is taking a spin around the
block. The engine and the entire chassis need to be brought
up to operating temperature, and need to operate that way
for a while. Ten or twenty miles is a must, and some of it
should be at highway speed. If you have air conditioning,
turn it on for a while to lube the seals, regardless of the
season.

> *Is there one single thing you can
> do to keep your very special car
> in the best possible condition?
> Yes. Drive it!*

But what if driving the car is just not practical? What if
your car must be stored for a long (consider anything over a
few months "long") period? Are there steps to minimize
deterioration? Yes.

First, all routine maintenance should be performed. This
includes lubricating the chassis, changing oil and filter, and
checking all fluid levels. There is some disagreement regard-

ing gasoline. Some people believe the tank should be topped off to prevent moisture from accumulating in the empty portion. Others prefer to leave the tank dry or with just a few gallons in it. A lot depends on how long the car is to be stored. If it's just over the winter, it probably doesn't matter, except having some fuel in the system makes more sense

Regular pump gasoline turns to a gel and leaves varnish accumulation throughout the entire system.

than leaving it bone dry. If it's for a longer period, there could be trouble. Regular pump gasoline eventually turns to a gel and leaves a varnish accumulation throughout the entire system. If this happens, there is no choice but to clean the whole system out.

There are some options. There are additives, such as one called *Sta-bil* designed to prevent fuel from going bad. Aviation fuel does not go sour, nor does "white" gas. The problem with both of these is finding them in your area or, in the case of aviation fuel, getting someone to sell it to you. Legally, you're supposed to pay road use tax on aviation fuel if it's used in a car. Some airports don't want to bother with the extra fuss for your few measly gallons. Despite the effort required, you should take some action to prevent sour gas from fouling a car you plan to store for some time.

You've heard the expression "stored on blocks" used. Should you bother? It depends. If your storage is just for the winter, you'd probably be better off leaving the car on its tires so it could at least be started and moved around in the garage conveniently. This isn't as good as an outside drive of several miles, but it beats cold storage. If storage is to be for

Right: A great way to keep an older car smelling fresh is the use of lemon-scented furniture polish on inside surfaces. Dave Burroughs leaves Pledge-coated rags and a lemon air freshener inside a closed car for a week to impart a fresh scent. Assuming there is no mold problem, a treatment like this will last for years.

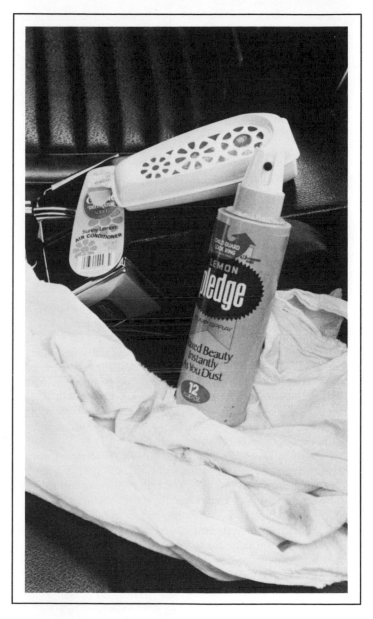

a longer period, then the car should definitely be blocked.

The purpose of blocking is not just to take weight off the tires. In fact, that is a side benefit. The purpose is to get the weight off the suspension, especially the bearings. And you don't have to suspend the car completely off the ground such that the tires aren't even touching. It varies with the type of car, but six inches of chassis elevation is normally adequate.

Speaking of tires, old car museums inflate them with nitrogen gas to reduce oxidation. A bit exotic, but it works. If you've got a relic with the original skins, it will be worth the trouble, particularly if the tires are tube-type.

It's a must to coat the interior cylinder walls with oil. There are two ways to do this, and you can play it super safe and do both. The first is to stall the car out by pouring oil in a slowly increasing volume into the carburetor. Sam Folz, the president of the *National Corvette Restorers Society* says a mixture of 50% kerosine and 50% *Casite* is used in his Michigan area to preserve stored boat engines, and it works well for cars too.

The other way to get lubricant into the cylinder walls is to remove the spark plugs and pour the oil right in. A few ounces are all that's required, and you can introduce it easily with an oil squirt can. Turn the engine over with the starter to distribute the oil with the plugs out, then replace the plugs. You can do the plug routine alone, or in combination with introducing oil into the carburetor. There are special devices that can be inserted into the spark plug holes in place of the plugs during storage which will absorb any moisture present in the cylinder chamber area.

The battery should be disconnected and, for longer storage periods, removed to a separate location entirely. It's a good idea to put a charge on it occasionally. There is an old gas station rule that has circulated for years stating that you never store a battery on concrete, but some people claim to do it without a problem. Suit yourself.

Whether or not your car has its original battery, you might want to consider buying a guaranteed-for-life battery to just leave in the car for convenient starting. A few years ago, these batteries were very popular and were available from several sources. Apparently the companies selling them concluded they weren't such a good idea, because only a few still sell them. The guarantee on these batteries was perfect for a collector car person. As long as you own your car, they keep giving you a new battery whenever yours fails. At this writing, *Penneys* still had them available.

If you can find dehydrant packets of the type packaged with electronic gear and cameras, put a few into the interior. If there is cloth inside, moth balls are a good idea. An open box of baking soda is also recommended. You can freshen the interior with an air freshener, but don't leave it in there for an extended period. A week is sufficient.

John Amgwert puts a box of *D-Con* mice killer in the engine compartment and interior of each car he stores. John has seen interiors ruined by mice, and has had mice build a nest in the air cleaner of one of his own cars.

Radiators are another subject of controversy. Our preference is to flush them thoroughly before storage and fill with a high quality antifreeze mixed with distilled water. Some pros prefer storing cars with the cooling systems drained.

John Amgwert puts a box of mice killer in the engine compartment and interior of each stored car.

If the car is a convertible, the top should be left up. The windows should be left up too, but with an inch or so opening at the top. Again, some experts disagree and put the windows up snug. The car should definitely be covered, but the cover must be one that breathes. If nothing else, use a couple of old cotton sheets.

Ideal storage prevents any sunlight from entering the storage area, which should be humidity controlled. Obviously, the combination of high humidity and darkness makes for ideal mold growth conditions. Tires should always be covered.

When a car is stored but started occasionally, a new exhaust system can rot out in short order due to condensation forming. Don Williams minimizes this problem by drilling a small drain hole in the lowest part of the muffler. In the case of his Corvettes, this is at the rear tip of the muffler.

Restarting a car that's been stored properly isn't always easy. Normally, the engine will turn for a while without firing due to the oil in the cylinders. Often, it is necessary to remove and clean the oil-drenched plugs. There are quick-start products available which are squirted directly into the carburetor. But care should be exercised in using them. Some people maintain they're not especially good for engines, and they are extremely flammable and therefore somewhat dangerous. An engine in good working order shouldn't need this assist.

There are a couple of specific things that concern practically anyone who has a car that is stored or used infrequently. Some of these things are important for frequently-used cars as well, especially if they fall into the collector category.

Mix the best unleaded with the best leaded, and the resulting octane is higher than either.

The first topic is gasoline. It's no secret that real premium auto fuel is a thing of the past. So what if your car is a high compression model requiring high octane? Well, the aviation fuel mentioned earlier works well. Standard avgas is either 87 octane or 100 octane, and it's good stuff. It is expensive and probably difficult or inconvenient to obtain. But all things considered, there is no better solution for an ultra-high compression car.

Shell Oil Company has a recommendation. They say that if you mix the best leaded fuel you can find with the best no-lead premium, you'll wind up with a fuel that has a higher octane than either of the fuels alone. This isn't voodoo, but has instead to do with some strange reactions the lead molecules have with the premium unleaded.

Is there a problem running unleaded or low-lead fuels in a car designed during the leaded period? Not too much. Unleaded tends to run hotter and this can burn exhaust valves prematurely. But the low-lead blend should work fine, and by the time leaded fuel no longer is available, someone will have a fix on the market. Here's the catch. Some fuel lines don't hold up as long when exposed to no-lead or gasohol fuels. There isn't a heck of a lot you can do about it, but be aware of the potential problem, and buy the right kind of replacement hose if it comes to that.

Another area of concern is oil. You've heard the old business about oil never wearing out, just getting contaminated. There's a lot of truth to that. But the kind of driving that "special" cars get is usually the worst in terms of oil contamination. If your car has a recommended oil change interval of 4000 miles and you drive it 500 miles a year, don't plan on changing oil every eight years. Compared to the value of your car, an oil change is cheap. If you drive it at all, or even if you just start if occasionally (especially then) change the oil and filter at least twice a year. So it looks nice and clean when it drains. Why risk the health of your machine for the cost of an oil change?

Corrosion of brake components is another major problem for cars which are stored or not driven regularly. Some cars have chronic brake problems whether they are driven or not. Ironically, one of the best braking systems ever devised was for the 1965 Corvette. This four-wheel disc system has continued almost unchanged to this day. The irony is that Corvette disc brake systems have been extremely troublesome for owners. Even if you don't own a Corvette, the lessons

---

The irony is that Corvette disc brake systems have been extremely troublesome for owners.

---

learned by the Corvette market and the fix that is now available to Corvette owners is informative and useful.

The major brake problem owners of 1965 and newer Corvettes experienced was leakage of fluid in the calipers, specifically around the seals of the pistons. The Corvette disc brake system uses four pistons at each wheel, so each car has sixteen pistons in all. Keeping all sixteen properly sealed should have been a high priority of the engineers who designed the system, but some critical errors were apparently made. Most fundamental was the choice of materials. The piston material was anodized aluminum, but the caliper housing was nodular cast iron on early cars, and grey cast iron on later models. If the anodizing comes off the piston there are electrolytic reactions between the iron and the aluminum. But the real root of the problem is that iron rusts.

This isn't a problem seen only in cars driven through a dozen salt-laden northern winters.

In the Corvette system, what happened was that as the brake pads wore, the pistons moved toward the pads, occupying new positions in the bore of the iron caliper housing. Previously, this portion of the bore had not been protected from the elements, and the piston seal then ceased sealing as it came upon a rusted or corroded area. This isn't a problem seen only in Corvettes driven through a dozen salt-laden northern winters. This was a problem very common to Corvettes all over the country. Neither was it a problem common only to high-mileage models. The truth was that it was common to all Corvettes with four-wheel discs.

Corvette owners had to contend with what could be called "typical" brake problems . . rust-through of a line, condensation within the system, frozen bleeder screws, and so on. All this added to the tremendous problem of leaking calipers at the piston bores made for a very frustrating problem. Especially frustrating because for a long time there was no permanent cure. The bores could be honed out and a new set of seals installed around the pistons. By this time the pads had been soaked with fluid and had to be replaced. If corrosion was too severe, the calipers, pistons, pads, and seals all had to be replaced. The latter was a very expensive proposition. The maddening part was that both cures were not cures at all, just temporary fixes. The corrosion just started all over again.

Two things changed the picture. First was the introduction by some enterprising entrepreneurs of Corvette brake calipers sleeved in stainless steel, and solid stainless steel pistons. Caliper cylinder wall corrosion became a thing of the past. One of the leaders of the stainless steel brake field, the *Stainless Steel Brakes Corporation* in Clarence, New York, even added stainless steel bleeders and special tapered shim kits to eliminate wheel bearing and rotor run-out which could lead to a spongy pedal condition. Going with a complete system such as offered by *Stainless Steel Brakes Corporation* (and others such as *Dr. Vette*) not only puts the Corvette system in like-new condition, it keeps it there indefinitely. Especially if the second of the two magic fixes is employed.

The second fix is silicone brake fluid. Without doubt, any car worthy of collector car status deserves a switch to silicone fluid. Its main advantage is that it is not compatible with water. It won't hold water. Conventional brake fluid soaks up water and water causes corrosion. Silicone fluid has another nice feature in that it won't hurt most finishes if accidently spilled. If you've ever dribbled regular brake fluid on a fender, you know what it will do.

Changing to silicone requires a complete flush of the braking system. In the case of a Corvette, a change to stainless steel calipers is an ideal time to make the switch to silicone fluid. For any other car, it is suggested that the brake system be flushed with alcohol, then with silicone fluid until every trace of the old petroleum-based fluid is gone.

As we mentioned in the beginning of the text, most of the tips mentioned were personal favorites of the experts we consulted, but that doesn't mean that other techniques don't exist. There is, after all, a considerable variance in what different owners seek from their cars and, of course, the cars themselves. But the techniques discussed do work and work well. Perhaps by meshing them with your own time-proven techniques, you can make that special car even more so.

ORDER FORM

Send_____copies of
SECRETS OF THE SHOW CARS
@ **$6.95** each ....$_____._____
                              Postage/Handling _____1.50_____
                    Check/Money Order Enclosed$_____._____

NAME _____
STREET _____
CITY _____STATE_____ZIP_____

Mail Order to: **Michael Bruce Associates, Inc.**
                 Post Office Box 396
                 Powell, Ohio 43065

ORDER FORM

Send_____copies of
SECRETS OF THE SHOW CARS
@ **$6.95** each ....$_____._____
                              Postage/Handling _____1.50_____
                    Check/Money Order Enclosed$_____._____

NAME _____
STREET _____
CITY _____STATE_____ZIP_____

Mail Order to: **Michael Bruce Associates, Inc.**
                 Post Office Box 396
                 Powell, Ohio 43065

ORDER FORM

ORDER FORM